Pollock

French edition:
© 1997 Éditions Cercle d'Art, Paris
Editor: Jean-Luc Chalumeau

English edition:
© 2003 Ediciones Polígrafa, S. A.
Balmes, 54 - 08007 Barcelona

© 2003 Jackson Pollock. VEGAP, Barcelona
English translation: Josephine Watson
I.S.B.N.: 84-343-1005-8
Dep. legal: B. 9892 - 2003
Printed by Filabo, S. A., Barcelona

Jackson Pollock

Ediciones Polígrafa

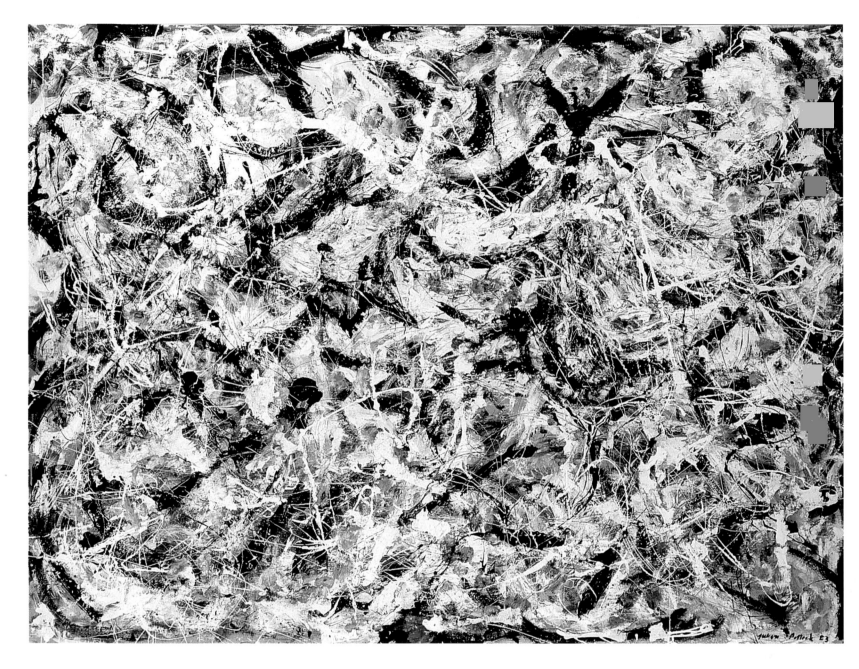

Greyed Rainbow, *1953.*
Oil on canvas, 182.8 × 243.8 cm.
The Art Institute, Chicago.

The Oeuvre of Pollock in the Context of the 20th Century

One of the most repeated clichés regarding Jackson Pollock portrays him as the pioneer of an exclusively American art, no longer indebted to any European legacy. This is what Irving Sandler has especially endeavoured to prove, in his book *The Triumph of American Painting*, a title certainly devoid of ambiguity. Such an interpretation however, takes into account neither the true contents of the works, nor Pollock's own statements, who said on the subject: "The idea of an isolated American painting, so popular in this country during the thirties, seems absurd to me, just as the idea of creating a purely American mathematics or physics would seem absurd… And, in another sense, the problem doesn't exist at all; or, if it did, would solve itself: an American is an American and his painting would naturally be qualified by that fact, whether he wills it or not. But the basic problems of contemporary painting are independent of any one country."

Pollock's Sources

As in the case of all artists, Pollock's work obviously received influences and while it's true that he was a master of the dripping technique, so it is that the art critic Clement Greenberg attributed its paternity to Hans Hofmann, a friend of the painter. During the thirties Pollock was deeply impressed by the work of the Mexican muralist Orozco (fig. a) and subsequently by Joan Miró, Max Ernst and André Masson (fig. b), all of whom had established themselves in New York in the forties. Yet according to his wife Lee Krasner, Picasso was "the only master that truly counted for him, the master he always wished to measure himself against."[1] Up until 1946 Pollock, as De Kooning, could be defined as a late Cubist, although by then he had already begun to distance himself from Cubist space which, both nourished and subverted by the contributions of Miró (fig. c), Siqueiros and Orozco, would be subjected, in Pollock's case, to a passion revealing a violently Expressionist temperament. Moreover, Greenberg observed that paintings such as *The She-Wolf* (fig. 12) "borrow Picassian ideas, experimenting them with an eloquence and strength that Picasso would never have granted them."

In the autumn of 1944 Pollock first tried his hand at chisel engraving, under the tuition of Hayter at the famous Atelier 17, which had moved from Paris to New York because of the war. Quite likely, the example set by this master imbued with the "vital character of line itself" and the dangers inherent in the use of the chisel completely released his own lines, which would soon unfold in an independent, bold and seemingly automatic fashion. From the mid forties on, Pollock explored what he termed "non-objectivity", that consisted, according to his own personal vocabulary, of "veiling the image". In other words, as opposed to the Surrealists, who conceived the unconscious as a source of images to be depicted, Pollock must have felt closer to the attitude of André Masson, another assiduous visitor to Atelier 17, whose oeuvre he was quite familiar with. Masson transcribes unconscious drives without attempting to illustrate them, although as we shall see later, in Pollock's case things are more complex.

A Truly Pictorial Revolution

During the winter of 1946–1947, thanks to the drip technique and more specifically to his work entitled *Cathedral* (fig. 19), Pollock radically displaces the issues raised by the painting of his day. Line becomes coloured form and invades the angles of the picture while respecting its limits, for the painter's gesture is repeated when approaching the contours. An initial monochrome mark forms the first "image", the master figure; then, complicated usually elliptic traces are employed to "expose" it in several successive stages. It is like transferring to painting the

a. *José Clemente Orozco*
Alegoría nacional, *1947-1948.*
Fresco with incisions made by the Escuela Normal de México. Total surface: 380 m².

b. *André Masson*
Enchevêtrements, *1941.*
Tempera and sand on cardboard, 41 × 32 cm.

c. *Joan Miró*
Towards the Rainbow, *1941.*
From the Constellation Series
Gouache and oil wash on paper, 45.8 × 38 cm.
The Jacques and Natasha Gelman Collection.

1. Conversation between Lee Krasner-Pollock and Jean-Luc Chalumeau, Antenne 2, 1979.

d. *Pablo Picasso*
Reclining Nude under a Starry Sky, 1936.
Oil on canvas, 130.5 × 162 cm.

e. *Pollock, 1949. Photo: Arnold Newman.*

f. *Kenneth Noland, 1982. Photo: Harvey Stein.*

technique of re-recording developed at the time by great jazzmen such as Charlie Parker, John Coltrane and Dizzie Gillespie, who play their own recordings a number of times in a row, "one on top of another". In this sense, Pollock's painting is absolutely in tune with its age.

Finally, the pictorial fabric is completely covered by interacting colours, following laws that differ from the traditional laws governing value contrast. Greenberg has written that pictorial art in the West created the illusion of the third dimension thanks to contrasting values rather than to the use of perspective. There is "depth" in Pollock, but it is already an exclusively pictorial depth. The abandonment of the laws of value contrast does in fact launch a pictorial revolution: colours are no longer "formal" — as they continue to be in Picasso — but "anti-formal". This has led the philosopher Jean-François Lyotard to see in Pollock's works the movement of desire itself, instead of its hallucinatory object. The object of desire would have been suppressed to the exclusive benefit of the sheer desire to paint.

The "Return" of the Figure

The drip paintings of the years 1947 to 1950 prove that after many lengthy trials, Pollock managed to bring together and integrate in his dramatic gestures all notions of composition, drawing, shape and colour. To do so he required a certain degree of violence combined with knowledge: a paroxysm of painting impossible to keep up indefinitely. Following the great 1950 exhibition at the Museo Correr in Venice, Pollock, at the peak of his glory, was unable to make further progress in the same direction. The creative brevity of his aesthetic trajectory reminds us of Van Gogh, as Pollock similarly suffered bouts of extreme anxiety that account for his frequent internments in psychiatric hospitals. Much has been said of his return to representation in the works produced between 1951 and 1954, works in which one can almost always discern figures similar to those depicted by Picasso (fig. d). Many hold the opinion, Lee Krasner among them, that Pollock did never in fact abandon representation. All that happened was that in the period stemming from 1947 to 1950, he managed to completely disguise the obsessive Picassian images under no end of signs. The urge to conceal the figure is what makes Pollock an Abstract Expressionist, an urge particularly evident in the ritual dance performed by the artist around and on top of the canvas, stretched over the ground, for he has no qualms about moving all over it (fig. e). Nonetheless, his hidden figures were destined to reappear with irrepressible force once the artist's physical and mental strength began to wane.

"A Line that Bounds and Delimits Nothing"

In 1993 Rosalind Krauss formulated the following question in *Cahiers du Musée national d'art moderne*: "Who's afraid of Greenberg's Pollock?" This question evoked the theses of those psychologists for whom "the pregnancy of a shape is the strength it derives from its simplicity, from its ability to impose itself as a shape. In order to be perceptible the shape needs to be able to be projected on a frontal plane opposite, in other words, on a vertical plane." This ideal sketch — respected by Pollock's heirs in the field of painting, Helen Frankenthaler, Morris Louis, Kenneth Noland (fig. f) and Jules Olitski — Krauss stresses, has allowed the critic Michael Fried to take Greenberg's statement to its ultimate consequences, according to which Pollock's abstract line "bounds and delimits nothing except eyesight."

As a result, any return to representation, albeit partial, could only be regarded as an unacceptable regression by Clement Greenberg and the formalist critics who were only interested in seeing and studying Pollock's "grand period."

Rosalind Krauss has insisted on the fact that between 1951 and 1952 the black and white paintings containing figures, often barely recognisable, were not interpreted as a change of direction by the most lucid critics, who challenged the unbearable alternative that the artist was often obliged to accept, against his will, according to which firstly, abstraction lacks a thematic motif and is therefore mere decoration, and secondly, the motif necessarily leads to the representation of an object. In fact, Pollock's ambition to paint nothing is comparable to the aspirations of Mondrian and Malevich, who dreamt of painting the Void, or in other words, the Self — the purified Self discussed by Hegel — and this is what we must bear in mind if we wish to contemplate Pollock's works from the appropriate perspective.

The World and Discoveries of Pollock

g. *Willem de Kooning*
Woman II, *1952.*
Oil on canvas, 150 × 109.3 cm.

A famous dispute brought the champions of two different theses regarding the nature of Pollock's discoveries in his most fertile period, from 1947 to 1950, face to face. Harold Rosenberg expounded his theory in an article entitled "The American Action Painters" published in *Art News* in December 1952, while Clement Greenberg made his stance public in an article published ten years later, in December 1962, in the review *Encounter* under the title "How Art Writing Earns Its Bad Name".

Painting as Action?

Harold Rosenberg came up with the generic term Action Painting to describe the activity of several North American painters, among them Willem de Kooning (fig. g) and Franz Kline, although the model for Action Painters was most certainly Jackson Pollock. Thinking precisely of the latter's progression, he coined other terms including the picture surface as an "arena", the picture as an "event". For Rosenberg, Pollock's painting is above all else "an act", and therefore something "inseparable from the artist's biography . . . Action Painting . . . has removed all separation between art and life." So, in essence, the work is defined by the procedure employed by the artist or, if you prefer, by his way of becoming psychically involved in the drip process, instead of by the end result. The latter was characterised by Rosenberg as "metaphysical wallpaper", an expression lacking all pejorative connotations yet one that was deemed unfortunate, to say the least, by Clement Greenberg, for he found it hard to believe that Pollock's originality was reduced exclusively to Action Painting.

According to Greenberg, Pollock's canvases, insofar as they hung on the wall, should be considered paintings, independent entities that could be studied abiding by formal grounds, just as any other work of art. The fact of the canvas having been stretched over the floor to be painted was therefore of little consequence. In a famous essay, "Modernist Painting", published in *Arts Yearbook* in 1962, the critic applied his valuation method to Pollock's pictures, proving the birth of a specific type of space that responded to the conditions of what he termed modernist painting. According to Greenberg, the works from the significant 1947–1950 period (fig. h) attained a synthesis between the objective flatness of the canvas and the illusion of painting inasmuch as they proposed a concrete space. Pollock's genius consisted in his invention of a space deliberately confined to the initial flatness of the support. By preventing the identification of the objects delimited in the pictorial field, Pollock's marks had abolished the traditional relationships between "figure" and "background".

h. *Jackson Pollock*
Galaxy, *1947.*
Oil, aluminium paint and small gravel on canvas, 110.4 × 86.3 cm. Joslyn Art Museum, Omaha, Nebraska. Gift of Miss Peggy Guggenheim.

"All but Naïve"

Greenberg marvelled at the double quality of Pollock's linear entwinements, for they suggested at once impenetrability and openness. This is what occurs for instance, in *One* (fig. 33), often cited as the artist's great masterpiece, where the gaze is induced to carry out an endless exploratory journey into a new third dimension: "a strictly optical third dimension . . . in which and through which one can only look and travel with one's eyes."

Greenberg's theories were subsequently called into question, especially by Rosalind Krauss, yet beyond all interpretations one fact remains: the world of Jackson Pollock is all but naïve. Its complexity obeys, in the first instance, the fact that this painting integrates multiple sources (fig. i), sources stemming from all periods and civilisations. As Lee Krasner has said, Pollock's painting certainly implies "a cross section in world history".

i. *Pablo Picasso*
The Kitchen, *1948.*
Oil on canvas, 175 × 252 cm. Musée Picasso, Paris.

The Life of Jackson Pollock

j. *The Pollock family in 1917.*

k. *Jackson Pollock at the age of sixteen.*

l. *Jackson Pollock*
Composition with Woman, *1938-1941.*

1912 Paul Jackson Pollock is born on the 28th of January, the fifth child in the family formed by LeRoy (Roy) Pollock and Stella May McClure, who live on Watkins Ranch in Cody (Wyoming).

1913 The Pollocks purchase a farm in Phoenix (Arizona).

1922–1927 Changes of residence are frequent. At the age of eleven Jackson Pollock is initiated into the traditions of the Indian culture of Arizona (fig. l).

1927 Jackson attends Riverside High School, but does not find it easy to follow the classes.

1928 The family settles in Los Angeles and Pollock enrols at the Manual Arts High School where he will meet Philip Guston.

1930 Pollock discovers the latest fresco paintings by Orozco at Pomona College (California). He moves to New York with his brothers Frank and Charles, where he will attend evening classes organised at the Art Students League, imparted five days a week by Thomas Hart Benton. He meets the painter Orozco.

1931 Having made friends with his professor Thomas Benton, Jackson Pollock will spend the summer at his house.

1932 Pollock travels around the United States, hitch-hiking. He discovers the frescoes by Siqueiros at the Chouinard Art School. Upon his return he is accepted as an assistant teacher at the Art Students League, thus saving his own enrolment fee. In December Benton leaves the League, while Pollock will become a fully-fledged member. He produces lithographs that will be published by Theodore Wahl in 1934.

1933 His father dies. Jackson Pollock tries his hand at sculpture during the summer, and is present when Diego Rivera produces his frescoes for the New Yorker's School.

1934 Pollock travels again around the States, this time driving an old Model T Ford and accompanied by his brother Charles, himself a painter.

1935 On the 1st of August Pollock is hired by the Federal Arts Project of the Works Progress Administration (Easel Division), a section of the National Recovery Program launched by Roosevelt. This is a project devised and carried out by the government to give work to artists and to introduce art into public buildings.

1936 Siqueiros opens an experimental studio in New York known as the Laboratory of Modern Techniques in Art. Jackson and his brother Sanford, also an artist, are invited to take part in the activities, that include air-gun painting as well as the use of industrial synthetic materials (shellac and Duco). Pollock meets Lenore (Lee) Krasner.

1937 Pollock begins to receive psychiatric treatment to cure his addiction to alcohol. He meets the art critic John Graham, after having read with interest his study entitled "Primitive Art and Picasso", published in the review *Magazine of Art*.

1938 The artist loses his job as a result of his repeated absences, and is subsequently admitted into the New York Hospital for detoxification. Although he will resume his activity in the easel painting section of the Federal Arts Project his salary will be lower.

1939 Under the direction of Doctor Joseph Henderson, Pollock submits himself to therapy based on Jungian psychoanalysis, in which his drawings are used as a therapeutic resource.

1941 Doctor Henderson leaves New York. Pollock continues his treatment under the Jungian practitioner Violet Staub de Laszlo.

1942 The artist takes part in an exhibition organised by John Graham at McMillan Inc., bringing together American artists of the École de Paris, alongside Matisse, Picasso, De Kooning and Lee Krasner, who introduces Pollock to her professor, Hans Hofmann. Krasner and Pollock move into the New York apartment previously occupied by

Sanford when the latter leaves for Connecticut. Pollock's canvas *The Flame* of 1937 is displayed at the Metropolitan Museum of Art in the exhibition "Artists for Victory".

1943 Peggy Guggenheim invites Jackson Pollock and Robert Motherwell to make collages which will be included in an exhibition organised for the months of April and May at her gallery, Art of This Century. The canvas entitled *Stenographic Figure* is presented at the Spring Salon for Young Artists.
Peggy Guggenheim offers Pollock a contract, and commissions a mural painting for her hall. In November Pollock is the object of a one-man show at Art of This Century.

1944 Pollock is invited to take part in the Surrealist section of "Abstract and Surrealist Art in America", an exhibition organised by Sidney Janis for the Cincinnati Art Museum. The Museum of Modern Art in New York, under the directorship of Alfred Barr, acquires *The She-Wolf*, which thus becomes the first of Pollock's works to be purchased by a museum.

1945 Solo exhibitions of his work are held at Art of This Century and at The Arts Club of Chicago, where he presents *Guardians of the Secret*. In August the artist buys a farm in East Hampton (Long Island), and on the 25th of October he weds Lee Krasner (fig. m).

1946 Art of This Century houses his third solo exhibition, the same year that Pollock transforms the East Hampton farm into a studio. In December he takes part for the first time in the Annual Exhibition of Contemporary American Painting organised by the Whitney Museum of American Art (the "Whitney Annual").

1947 First drip paintings and last show at Art of This Century, which Peggy Guggenheim closes to return to Europe. Pollock signs a contract with Betty Parsons gallery, and holds his first exhibition there.

1948 Pollock takes part in the Venice Biennale XXIV, and undergoes further treatment to combat alcoholism.

1949 Year of his second show at Betty Parsons gallery.

1950 Jackson Pollock joins the group of painters defined by the press as "the irascibles," and which includes Baziotes, Gottlieb, Hofmann, De Kooning, Reinhardt and Rothko.
He is represented for the second time at the Venice Biennale XXV, and holds a solo exhibition at the Museo Correr in the Italian city.
In November he takes part in the show organised by Leo Castelli at Sidney Janis Gallery, where young American painters compete with French artists: Pollock's work confronts that of Lanskoy. The photographer Hans Namuth portrays the painter in his studio, both in still photographs and in film.

1951 Pollock resumes representational art. Michel Tapié presents one of his canvases at the show "Véhemences Confrontées" held at Galerie Nina Dausset in Paris. The artist submits himself to chemotherapy to cure his alcoholism. In the months of November and December he holds his fifth one-man show at Betty Parsons gallery.

1952 His exhibitions this year include a participation in the group show "Regards sur la peinture américaine", held at the Parisian Galerie de France, and the one-man show "Jackson Pollock 1948–1951" at Studio Facchetti. He signs a contract with Sidney Janis Gallery, where he will hold his first solo exhibition in November.

1953 The Musée d'Art Moderne of Paris includes his work in the show "12 Peintres et Sculpteurs Américains Contemporains", organised by the International Program of the Museum of Modern Art in New York.

1954 Clement Greenberg considers Pollock's solo exhibition at Sidney Janis Gallery a failure, stating in bad faith that "Pollock has lost his verve", as Rosalind Krauss recalls.

1954-1955 Pollock breaks his ankle and practically stops painting. In the summer of 1955 he resumes psychoanalysis for another stretch of time, and in the months of November and December holds a mini retrospective show at Sidney Janis Gallery, entitled "15 Years of Jackson Pollock".

1956 At 10.15 of the night of the 11th of August Jackson Pollock dies at the wheel of his car, after crashing into a tree. The exhibition of twenty-five paintings organised by Andrew Carnduff Ritchie for the Museum of Modern Art in New York thereby becomes a posthumous tribute.

m. *Lee Krasner*
Self-Portrait, *1933.*

n. *Jackson Pollock and Lee Krasner in Long Island, around 1950.*

Assimilation of Influences

In 1937 Thomas Hart Benton, master and then friend of Jackson Pollock, explained in his teachings that a work of art "represents the sum of stylistic influences motivating the artist. Nevertheless, before gaining access to art, these influences must be assimilated in the work which, thereby reorganised, will formulate a new artistic statement." In his paintings of the period ranging from 1933 to 1946, Pollock proves he has learnt his lesson perfectly, and often betrays the influences inspiring his work, especially that of Picasso, as shown in *Stenographic Figure* (fig. 10).

Yet, if according to this period Pollock could be defined as a "late Cubist", this name proves excessively reductionist bearing in mind the scope of the sources he drank from. Barbara Rose declares that "it is very difficult to understand the work of a man who had created such a complex synthesis, inspired in prehistoric cave paintings, Byzantine mosaics, Persian manuscripts, Celtic illuminations, Oriental calligraphy and the art of the Renaissance and the Baroque, to mention only some of the forms integrated in his style." To this we must add that in the late thirties and early forties and as a result of undergoing psychoanalytical treatment, Pollock's work presents derivations from the unconscious side of images, as exemplified for instance in the paintings *The Moon-Woman Cuts the Circle* (fig. 13) and *The She-Wolf* (fig. 12). From the very beginning, Pollock's painting reveals an eminent culture, and nothing would prove more mistaken than interpreting the violence of his graphic work as an inherent feature of the "ignorant alcoholic cowboy" temperament occasionally attributed to him.

1

1 Untitled (Self-Portrait), *1931–1935.*
Oil on gesso on canvas, mounted on fibreboard, 184 × 13.3 cm.
L. S. Pollock Collection, New York.

An experimental work made during Pollock's youth, this self-portrait was presented by Jean Clair at the thematic Pollock exhibition held in the framework of the 1995 Venice Biennale. Clair hoped to prove that the great aspiration of Abstract Expressionism was to depict the human countenance, a thesis that became the object of much heated debate.

2   Untitled (Woman), *1935–1938.*
Oil on fibreboard, 35.8 × 26.6 cm.
L. S. Pollock Collection, New York.

3

3 Bird, *1938–1941.*
Oil and sand on canvas, 70.5 × 61.6 cm.
The Museum of Modern Art, New York.
Gift of Lee Krasner in memory of Jackson Pollock.

4

4 Untitled (Circle), *1938–1941.*
Oil on gesso on fibreboard, 32.2 × 30.5 cm.
The Museum of Modern Art, New York.
Gift of Lee Krasner in memory of Jackson Pollock.

5 Going West, *1934–1938.*
Oil on gesso on fibreboard, 38.3 × 52.7 cm.
National Museum of American Art,
Smithsonian Institution, Washington, D.C.

6

6 The Flame, *1937.*
Oil on canvas, mounted on fibreboard, 51.1 × 76.2 cm.
The Museum of Modern Art, New York. Enid A. Haupt Fund.

*"The flame invades the canvas just as heavy clouds invade those by
El Greco — wrote Hubert Damisch — in both cases these elements are
intended to provide the painter with a means of defining a space that
emerges from the pictorial work itself, rather than from the play of
linear co-ordinates. Even so, the strokes enliven matter that Pollock still
finds somewhat elusive. Later on, the artist's originality would consist
precisely in establishing a close relation between the gesture produced
over the canvas and the painterly matter that will merge into the
brushstrokes themselves, the necessary outcome."*

7

7 Birth, *1938–1941.*
Oil on canvas, 116.4 × 55.1 cm.
Tate Gallery, London.

8 Untitled (Naked Man), *1938–1941.*
Oil on plywood, 127 × 60.9 cm.
Private collection. Courtesy Robert
Miller Gallery.

Pollock's pictures of the thirties belong
to his so-called Regionalist style,
characterised by the influence of the
Mexican painters Orozco and
Siqueiros, prone to large-scale mural
compositions from which Pollock
specifically takes the treatment of
landscape.

8

9 Man, Bull, Bird, *1938–1941.*
Oil on canvas, 60.9 × 91.4 cm.
The Anschutz Collection, Denver, Colorado.

10 Stenographic Figure, *ca. 1942.*
Oil on linen, 101.6 × 142.2 cm.
The Museum of Modern Art, New York.
Mr. and Mrs. Walter Bareiss Fund.

In this 1942 "scribble" William Rubin perceives an anticipation of the abstract graphics that would soon unify Pollock's compositions with the help of a rhythmical articulation known as "all-over" painting. The figure alluded to in the title, at once a woman and an animal with claws, enables the artist to try out numerous psychological associations, while identifying at the same time the formal influence of the character with the pathetically raised arm in Picasso's Guernica of 1937, that had made such an impression on him.

11

12   The She-Wolf, *1943.*
Oil, gouache and plaster on canvas, 106.4 × 170.2 cm.
The Museum of Modern Art, New York.

"Before 1946–1947 — notes Bernice Rose — Pollock's works, such as those produced by the drip technique, responded in each case to a particular graphic conception, while their motifs were specifically mythological and symbolic and their style representational. Pollock was an abstract, symbolist creator of images, yet even so he revealed an extraordinary pictorial sensitivity, a rivalry between the desire to paint by means of large splashes of colour and the urge, no less intense, to paint primed surfaces of an essentially linear conception." In The She-Wolf *we discern the theme of the Minotaur and Pasiphaë, illustrating the duality of animal/human nature.*

11   Male and Female, *ca. 1942.*
Oil on canvas, 184.4 × 124.5 cm.
Philadelphia Museum of Art, Philadelphia.
Gift of Mr. and Mrs. H. Gates Lloyd.

According to William Rubin, one can maintain that the head on the right, with its violently executed features, belongs to a male, while the one on the left, with its delicate curly eyelashes, is that of a female. Yet, in spite of the painting's title, we must not read it as a coded work concealing two complete human beings, but rather as two anthropomorphic creatures produced over a long period of time that to a great extent end up exchanging genders. Pollock was acutely aware of the sexual ambiguity in the genetic make-up of human beings, an ambiguity often deeply repressed.

13

13 The Moon-Woman Cuts the Circle, *ca. 1943.*
Oil on canvas, 109.5 × 104 cm.
Musée national d'art moderne, Centre de Création Industrielle,
Centre Georges Pompidou, Paris. Donated by Frank K. Lloyd,
Paris, 1979.

This painting was presented at the first one-man-show of
Pollock's works held at Peggy Guggenheim's gallery, Art of This
Century, in 1943. As the artist had undergone Jungian
psychoanalysis from 1939 to 1942, the contents of the picture
gave rise to several different readings prompted by its presumed
Jungian sources. For Bryan Robertson, as inferred from his
remarks made in 1960, this work stemmed "quite clearly from a
Jungian interpretation of matriarchy in which the moon is the
matriarchal sphere." One year later, Lawrence Alloway pointed
out in his turn that Pollock's representational works "are not
preconceived, but improvised", which in his view gave more force
to the thesis according to which Pollock sought to create myths.
In 1967 William Rubin equally considered the symbolic images of
Pollock's early works as "myth creating", specifying however that
Henderson's conclusions "could have been applied (or not) to
children or to psychotics, but they did not take into account the
fact that Pollock produced art." Rubin concluded by suggesting
that placing a Jungian straightjacket on Pollock's pictures
"reduces their poetic resonance but does not explicitly declare
their meaning."

14   Guardians of the Secret, *1943.*
Oil on canvas, 122.9 × 191.5 cm.
San Francisco Museum of Modern Art, San Francisco.
Albert M. Bender Collection, Albert M. Bender Bequest Fund Purchase.

*William Rubin, as well as criticising the "Jungian" explanation of this
canvas put forward by Henderson, stresses the fact that the central part
of the picture, with its spread of calligraphy, heralds the more abstract
works of the sixties. "Without being at all matured, its wild and
recurrent prophetic articulation constitutes a radical attempt to produce
a more flowing lyrical configuration than those based on forms
stemming from geometric compositions, as illustrated by the general
sketch of* Guardians.*" As regards identification of the animal depicted in
the lower area of the work, Pollock told Lee Krasner that it was a dog,
and "obviously it is an image of the father". This led to the interpretation
in keeping with which the dog is on guard beside the mysterious central
region, a cryptogram of the unconscious designating the word "secret".
In Freudian yet not Jungian terms, such would be the painter's sexual
desire for his mother, a desire that cannot be confessed and is thus
repressed and relegated to his unconscious, while the dog represents the
father forbidding access to the "treasure". Similarly, the guardians in the
guise of sentries on either side embody the superego, according to Freud
the "police" of the spirit.*

15

15 The Water Bull (Accabonac Creek Series), *ca. 1946.*
Oil on canvas, 76.5 × 213 cm.
Stedelijk Museum, Amsterdam.

16 Alchemy, *1947.*
Oil, enamel, aluminium paint and string on canvas, 114.6 × 221.3 cm.
Peggy Guggenheim Collection, Venice.
The Solomon R. Guggenheim Foundation, New York.

We owe the title of this picture to Ralph Manheim, Jackson Pollock's
neighbour in East Hampton, who had translated texts on the Surrealists
and was interested in alchemy as was Matta, a frequent visitor to Pollock's
studio in 1942. The title certainly expresses the influence of the idea in
vogue at the time, according to which the artist is an alchemist who
transmutes pigment, a vile material, into art, a precious one.

The Plenitude of Abstract Expressionism

It is generally accepted that Pollock attained the summit of his art in the works entitled *One: Number 31* (fig. 33) and *Autumn Rhythm: Number 30, 1950* (fig. 32). 1950 was indeed an exceptionally fertile year in the artist's career, in which he completed thirty-two pictures, one tenth of his entire production. The delicacy of his traces and the harmony of the tonalities help to create a seemingly immense space, even though, contrary to his reputation, large formats do not appear frequently in his oeuvre. Art critic Pierre Restany has underlined the fact that this is where the union between "active" and "meditative" perspective characteristic of Abstract Expressionism comes fully to light. Restany also recalls that Harold Rosenberg had found in the works produced from 1947 to 1950 the fortunate synthesis of the gestural revolution championed by Action Painting (especially represented by Willem de Kooning), and of the mystical spirit of the New York school (embodied in the works of Mark Rothko and Ad Reinhardt in particular).

In Pollock, the Abstract Expressionist phase as such coincides with his use of the drip technique, a moment in which, according to the art historian Giulio Caro Argan, "he is aware of the essential place he occupies in the frenetic rhythm of ritual, aware he only truly exists in one single space — the canvas — the unbearable emptiness of which drives him to convulsive movement. Pollock paints by moving across his canvas spread out on the floor, which means he sees his work from above; the artist's rôle is that of demiurge: he triggers the action and controls it."

The photographs by Hans Namuth splendidly render Pollock's way of painting at this time. Thanks in effect to these images, Pollock became a legend in his own lifetime, a well-deserved reward if Argan was right when he declared that Pollock was the only artist who imperiously perceived the extreme transcendence of the historical time he was living in, and the only one who was able to render it pictorially: "As in the case of the great Romantic artists such as Blake, to be the bearer of a supreme message for humankind, extenuated by terrible crises, was Pollock's duty."

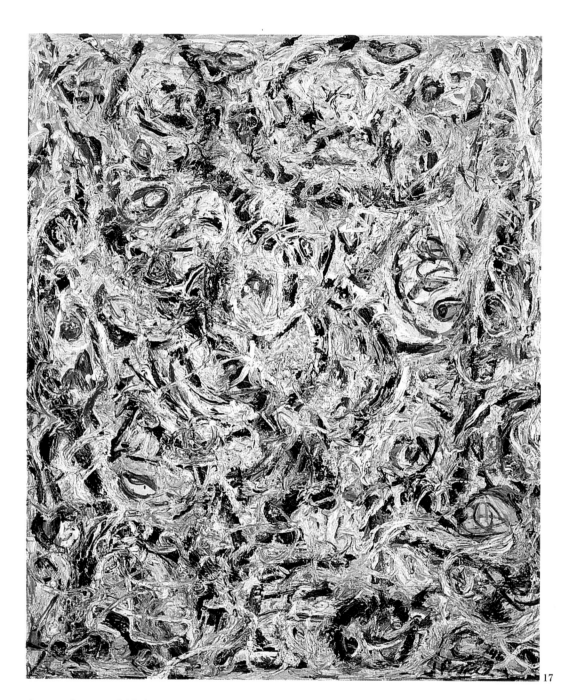

17

17   Eyes in the Heat
(Sounds in the Grass Series), *1946.*
Oil on canvas, 137.2 × 109.2 cm.
Peggy Guggenheim Collection, Venice.
The Solomon R. Guggenheim Foundation, New York.

18 Enchanted Forest,
1947.
Oil on canvas,
221.3 × 114.6 cm.
Peggy Guggenheim
Foundation, Venice.

18

21 Summertime, Number 9 A, 1948, *1948.*
Oil and enamel on canvas, 84.5 × 549.5 cm.
Tate Gallery, London.

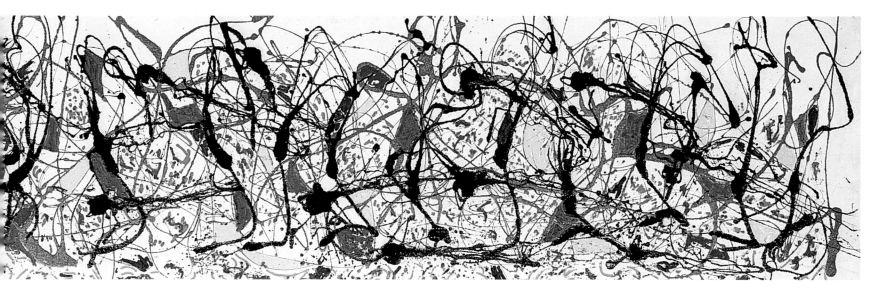

23 The Wooden Horse: Number 10 A, 1948, *1948.*
Oil, enamel and wood hobbyhorse on brown cotton canvas, mounted on
fibreboard, 90.1 × 190.5 cm.
Moderna Museet, Stockholm.

Despite having initiated his period dedicated to drip paintings, Pollock
would return to representational forms. Thus, the shape of a horse's head
amidst meshes of lines and stains is clearly suggested by the wooden
element attached to The Wooden Horse *of 1948 in the manner of collage,*
which led some commentators to seek "hidden imagery" in all Pollock's
drip paintings. Lee Krasner endorsed such investigations when she
quoted the words her husband uttered in front of her: "I choose to veil the
image." Yet for Pollock, the terms "image" and "imagery" merely
designated the first monochrome mesh covering his canvas, subsequently
flooded, to a greater or lesser extent, by the colours.

22

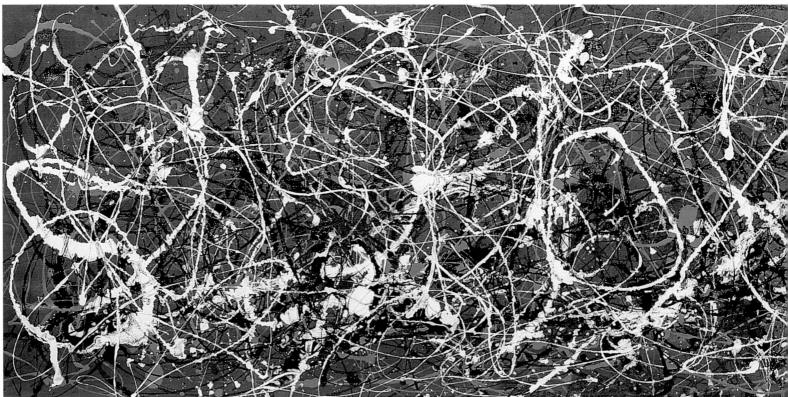

23

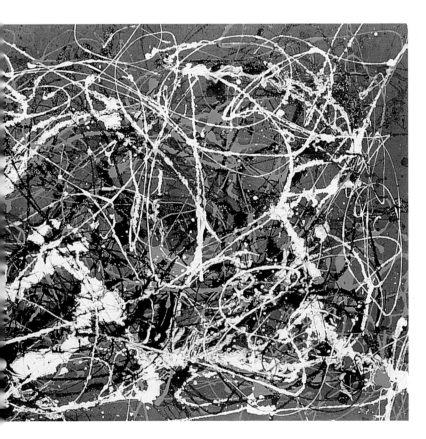

22 Number 13 A, 1948: Arabesque, *1948.*
Oil and enamel on canvas, 94.6 × 295. 9 cm.
Yale University Art Gallery, New Haven, Connecticut.
Gift of Richard Brown Baker, B.A., 1935.

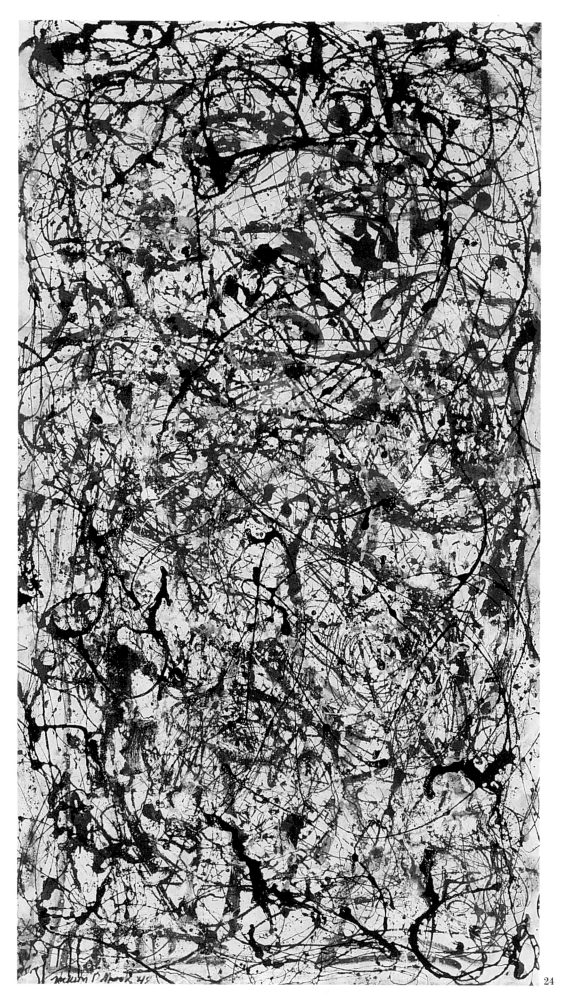

24 Number 26 A, 1948: Black and White, *1948.*
Enamel on canvas, 208 × 121.7 cm.
Musée national d'art moderne,
Centre de Création Industrielle,
Centre Georges Pompidou, Paris.

Pollock uses black and white in his own peculiar fashion. The material in this work — lacquer or industrial aluminium paint — is guided by the painter's gesture, following the balanced rhythm created by the black arabesques, the strokes of white, the splashes and reticles. The stains present the poles of attraction between which the different "woven" elements are placed. The fact of evenly filling up the entire pictorial surface liberates the artist from the problems deriving from the relationship between background and surface. We are no longer facing a way of seeing and reading but a movement of coloured line, what Michael Fried termed "optical space". The eye strays, it returns to the surface only to begin to explore ad infinitum the precarious threads of this palimpsest of sorts.

24

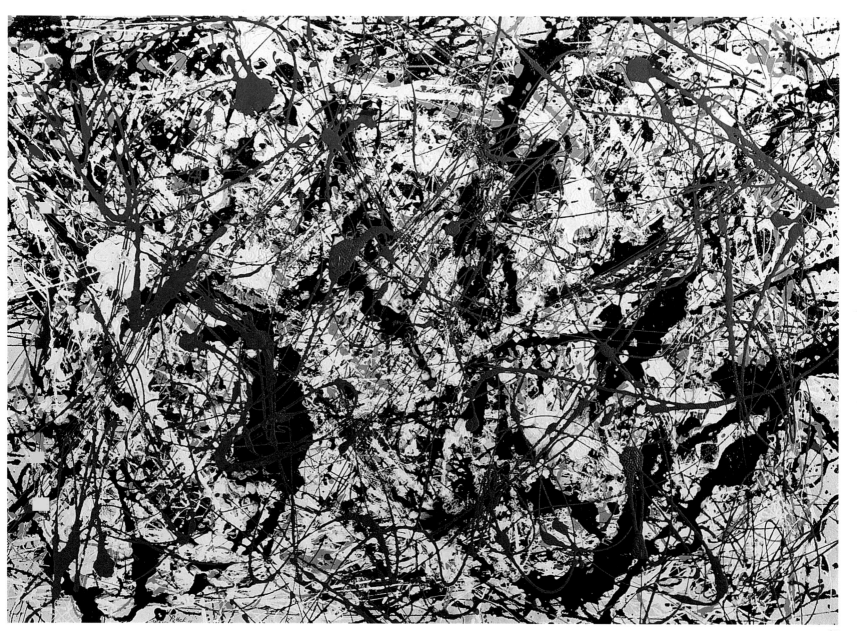

25   Silver over Black, Yellow and Red, *1948.*
Enamel on paper, pasted on canvas, 61 × 80 cm.
Musée national d'art moderne, Centre de Création Industrielle,
Centre Georges Pompidou, Paris.

This work is a fine example of an "all-over poured drip painting", to use the
terminology employed by American critics. The initial linear structure has been
poured over the paper — previously placed on the floor — in a swaying
movement, and then repeatedly covered or "veiled". The "initial image" which,
having inherited the sharp forms present in previous works, is perceived by
Pollock to be dangerous, has been "neutralised", according to the artist himself,
by the strokes comprised within the meshes of signs, that seem to possess enough
energy to exceed the very limits of the painting.

26 Number 13, 1949,
1949.
Oil, enamel and
aluminium paint on
gesso on paper,
mounted on fibreboard,
57.7 × 78.4 cm.
Private collection.

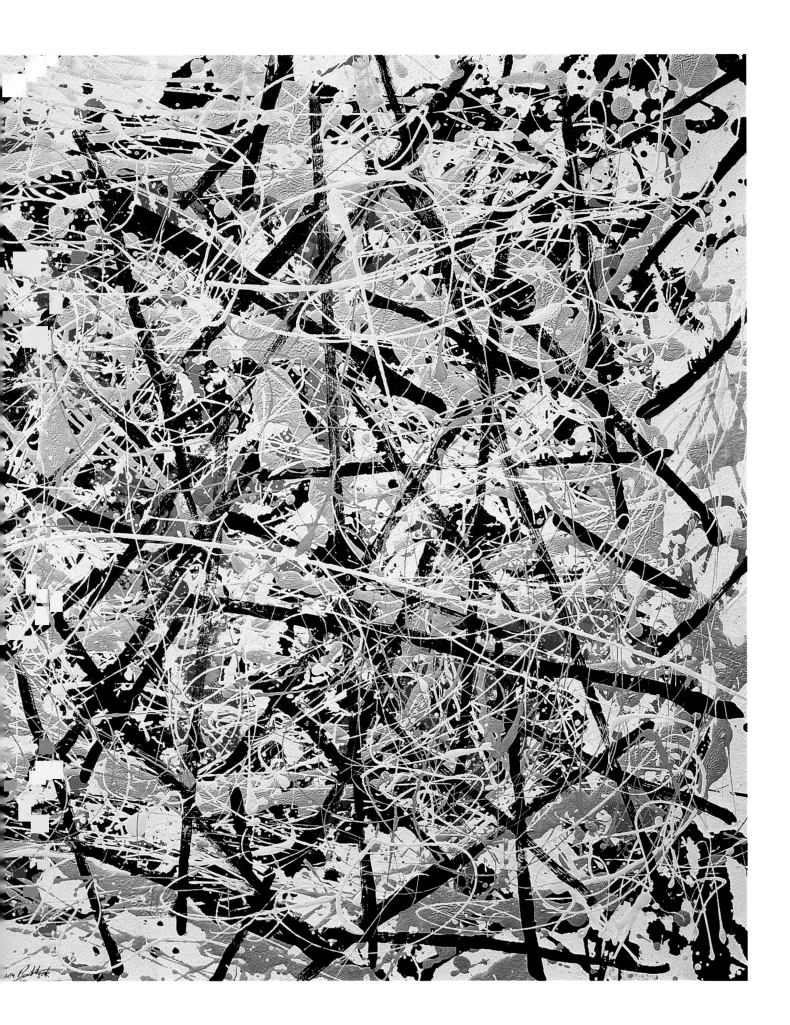

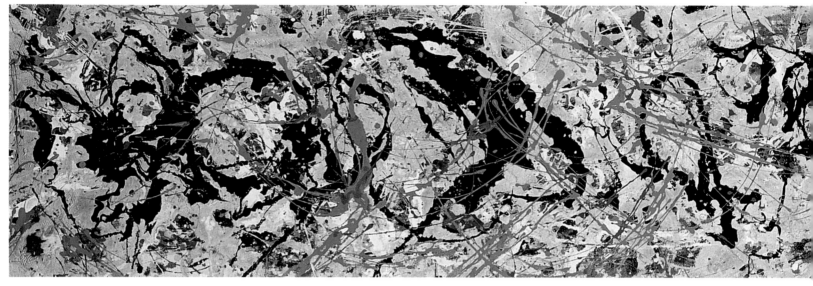

27 Number 10, 1949, *1949.*
Enamel and aluminium paint on canvas, mounted on wood,
45.7 × 272.4 cm.
Museum of Fine Arts, Boston.

Michael Fried's studies of Pollock's "non-objective" painting of the
years 1947–1950 have furthered our understanding of how the
artist approached the phenomenon of line departing from all
previous treatment: "Pollock's line, or the space in which it evolves,
has neither an interior nor an exterior . . . line in these paintings
is totally transparent, both in the non-illusionist space it occupies
yet does not structure, and in the impulses of a pure form of
energy, devoid of solidity, which seems to unfold without
resistance via these paintings . . . "

28

28 Number 8, 1949, *1949.*
Oil, enamel and aluminium paint on canvas,
86.6 × 180.9 cm.
Neuberger Museum of Art, Purchase College,
State University of New York. Gift of Roy R. Neuberger.

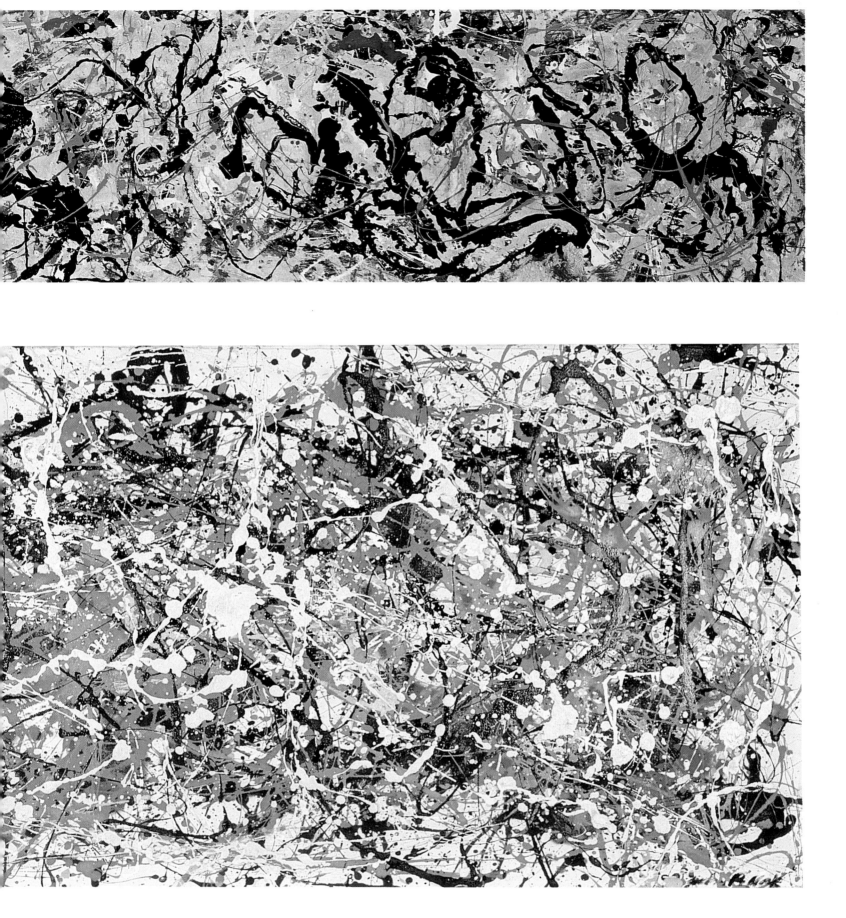

29

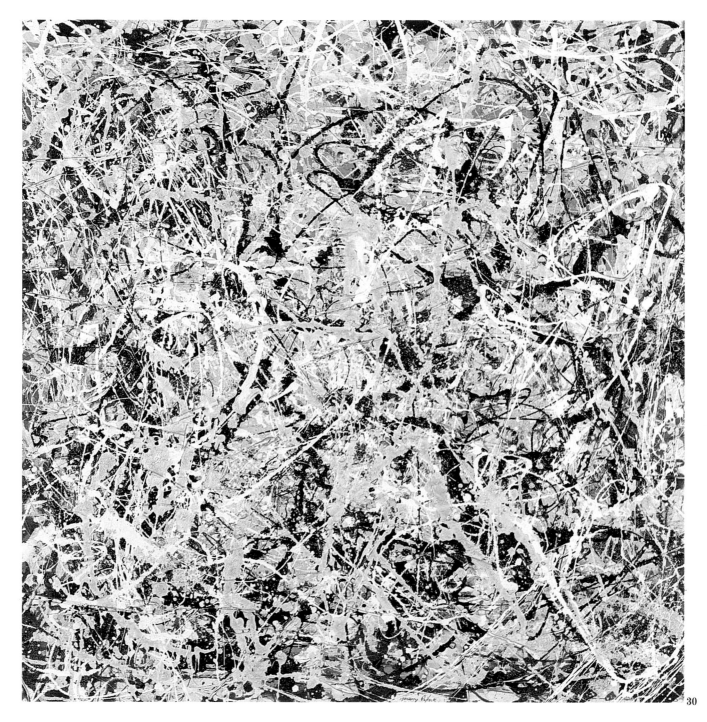

30

30 Number 4, 1949, *1949.*
Oil, enamel, aluminium paint and gravel on
canvas, mounted on fibreboard, 90.5 × 87.3 cm.
Yale University Art Gallery, New Haven.

29 Number 3, 1949: Tiger, *1949.*
Oil, enamel, aluminium paint, string and cigarette fragment
on canvas, mounted on fibreboard, 157.5 × 94.6 cm.
Hirshhorn Museum and Sculpture Garden,
Smithsonian Institution, Washington, D.C.
Gift of the Joseph H. Hirshhorn Foundation, 1972.

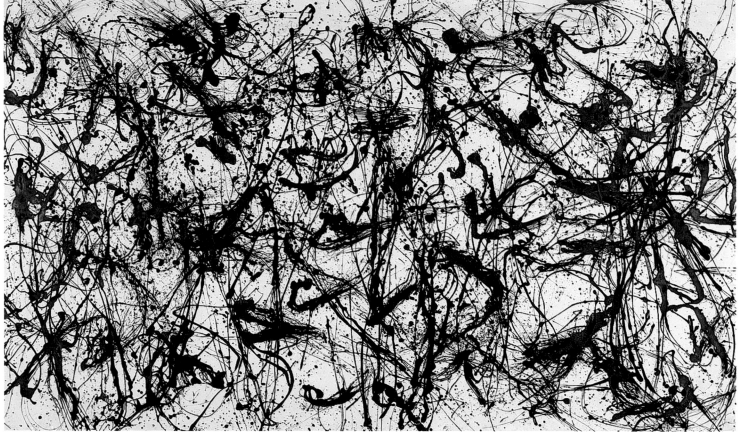

31

31 Number 32, 1950, *1950.*
Enamel on canvas, 269 × 457.5 cm.
Kunstsammlung Nordthein Westfalen, Düsseldorf.

This painting was made at the same time as Autumn Rhythm *and* One, *yet
its colourful visual highlights are much more vague than in the latter, writes
Bernice Rose, "leaving the striped black line nothing to attach itself to, thus
forcing it to merely form a descriptive outline." Exceptionally, Number 32
respects the first monochrome mesh — what Pollock called the initial image —
for the artist has refrained from going on to subsequent stages, usually based
on his covering the picture plane with complex splashes of coloured stains.*

32 Autumn Rhythm: Number 30, 1950, *1950.*
Oil on canvas, 267.7 × 525.8 cm.
The Metropolitan Museum of Art, New York. George A. Hearn Fund, 1957.

"For five years [Pollock] devoted himself frantically to this exercise [drip painting], producing a series of works characterised by a variety we find truly astonishing, bearing in mind the starting point of their creation. We are similarly amazed by the extraordinary pictorial quality of the simple black strokes, completely absorbed by the whiteness of the canvas, and by the highly complex webs, whose structure we must rediscover without losing sight of any single thread: Cathedral, 1947 . . . and the masterpiece One, 1950. Such strokes fly through the canvas, from side to side, forming a counterpoint that no longer unfolds in depth but in thickness, making sense only in connection with preceding strokes, for one colour follows another as if wishing to erase it . . . " Hubert Damisch, Les Lettres Nouvelles, *9/16 December 1959.*

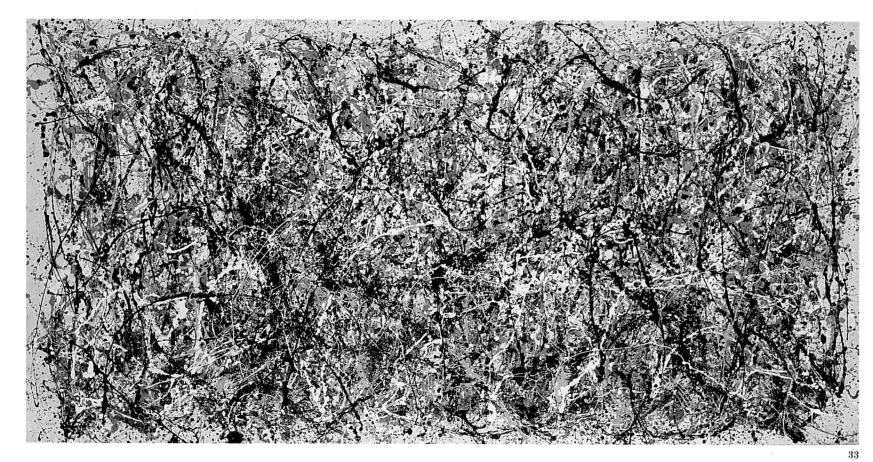

33 One: Number 31, 1950, *1950.*
Oil and enamel paint on canvas, 269.5 × 530.8 cm.
The Metropolitan Museum of Art, New York.

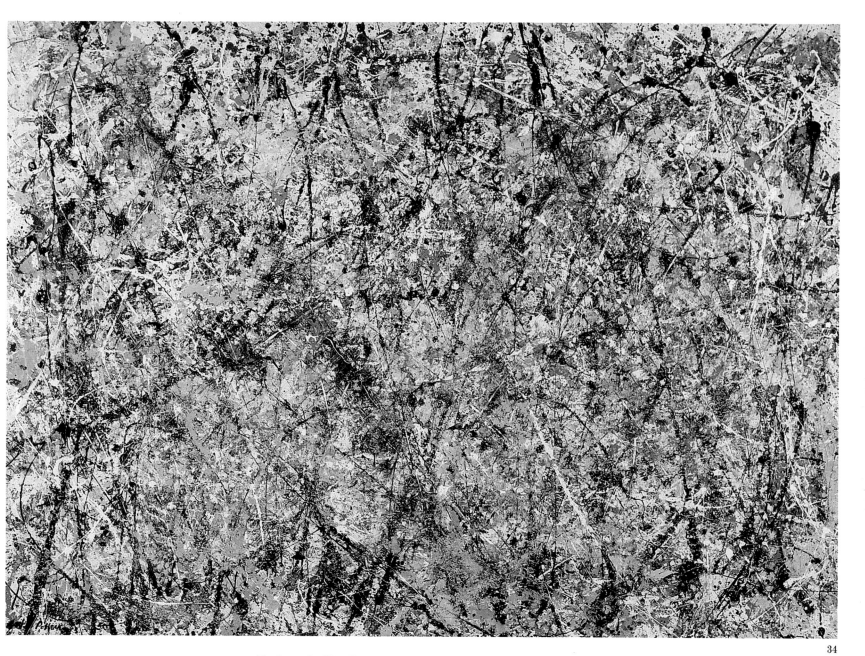

34 Lavender Mist: Number 1, 1950, *1950.*
Oil, enamel and aluminium paint on canvas, 221 × 299.7 cm.
National Gallery of Art, Washington, D.C. Ailsa Mellon Bruce Fund.

It is paradoxical that Clement Greenberg should have suggested the
term all-over apropos Pollock's large-scale drip paintings, and
Lavender Mist in particular: "'All-over' because their design repeats
itself all over the surface", specified the commentator. The very way
in which Pollock painted during this so-called 'classical' period
(1947–1951), in a sort of inspired dance around the canvas, has
furthered the idea that its edges arbitrarily delimited a surface
within the continuum of the painting. As if to avoid this
misunderstanding, Pollock included the print of his hand in three of
the sides of Lavender Mist, thereby marking the limits of the picture
and repeating in its interior his belief in the need for a 'frame'."
In point of fact, each drip painting betrays the rules of precise
composition, and consequently the term "all-over" proves
inappropriate.

35   Black and White Polyptych, *1950.*
Oil on canvas, 60.9 × 203.2 cm.
Mr. and Mrs. Arthur Rock.

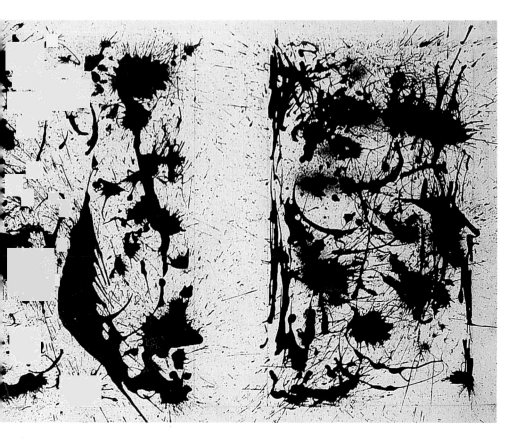

36

36   Number 11, 1951, *1951.*
Enamel on canvas, 146 × 352 cm.
Daros Collection, Switzerland.

37

37 Echo: Number 25, 1951, *1951.*
Enamel on canvas, 233.4 × 218.4 cm.
The Museum of Modern Art, New York. Acquired through
the Lillie P. Bliss Bequest and the Mr. and Mrs. David
Rockefeller Fund.

By 1951, Pollock's attitude regarding Abstract
Expressionism had clearly evolved. Reflecting upon the
problem of figure, in a hand-written note he observed:
"Abstract Expressionism doesn't worry me . . . and it is
certainly as 'non-objective' as it is 'non-representational'.
I'm very representational sometimes and I'm a little
representation always. But if you work from your
unconscious, shapes should emerge. We're all of us
influenced by Freud. I've been a Jungian for a long time . . .
To paint is a state of being . . . To paint is a discovery of
one's self. All good painters paint what exists."

38

38 Brown and Silver II, *1951.*
Enamel and silver paint on unprimed canvas, 144.7 × 107.8 cm.
Kunstmuseum Bern, Berne.

The Return to the Figure

During his years of training, between 1933 and 1946, Pollock's objectivity could be described as classical. His drip paintings of the years 1947–1951 correspond to his discovery of an ever-present "figure", yet one that was almost always illegible due to the density of successive floods of painting covering it. This figure is not representational: it is the first calligraphic mesh launched by the painter on to a pictorial surface. Apropos the works made between 1951 and 1953, in which he only employed the colour black, Daniel Abadie — curator of the Pollock exhibition held in Paris in 1982 — asked himself about the possible origin of the presence of small coloured stains that seemingly spoke of nostalgia, "of a need to take into account the emergence of the picture through its own means, instead of through the dripping procedure, an obsession he confronted in his last works." From 1951 onwards, Pollock abandoned dripping in favour of traditional paintbrushes. "At that point his oeuvre could only constitute an endeavour — and a failure to consciously reformulate the language he had afforded it." Only one true masterpiece would mark his last period, *The Deep* (fig. 44).

39

39 Out of the Web, Number 7, *1949.*
Oil and enamel on fibreboard, 121.5 × 244 cm.
Staatsgalerie Stuttgart, Stuttgart.

40

40 Easter and the Totem, *1953.*
Oil on canvas, 208.6 × 147.2 cm.
The Museum of Modern Art, New York.
Gift of Lee Krasner in memory of Jackson Pollock.

41   Blue Poles: Number II, 1952, *1952.*
Enamel and aluminium paint with glass on canvas,
210 × 486.8 cm.
National Gallery of Australia, Canberra.

42 Convergence: Number 10, 1952, *1952*.
Oil and enamel on canvas, 237.4 × 393.7 cm. Albright-Knox Art Gallery, Buffalo, New York.
Gift of Seymour H. Knox, 1956.

This picture presents a fine example of synthesis between an all-over abstract composition
and a background of black-and-white figures, above which the design appears variegated.

43 Portrait and a Dream, *1953.*
Oil on canvas, 148.6 × 342.2 cm.
Dallas Museum of Art, Dallas. Gift of Mr. and Mrs. Algur
H. Meadows and the Meadows Foundation, Incorporated.

A "psychoanalytical" canvas and, according to Flavio Caroli, the
most complex of all those painted by Pollock after the Second World
War, Portrait and Dream *combines something "truly visible" with*
something "truly dreamt". "If the dream is informel, *reality is*
deformed and the deformation is articulated over a vivisection of
the plastic planes — and their unfolding towards the foreground —
of a Cubist origin.

JACKSON POLLOCK 5

44

44 The Deep, *1953.*
Oil and enamel on canvas, 220.4 × 150.2 cm.
Musée national d'art moderne, Centre de
Création Industrielle, Centre Georges
Pompidou, Paris. Donated by The Menil
Foundation, Houston, 1975.

Shortly after the spring of 1951 Pollock
interrupted his work with the drip technique
— which he would resume on two occasions
in August 1952 — and strove to work on
monochromatic paintings. In this
remarkable work, the artist poured liquid ink
over the white canvas, as a result of which
the porosity of the cotton creates nuances
that give rise to "figures". The splashes are
not obtained by the use of sticks but of huge
syringes. This canvas is Pollock's
masterpiece where, as mentioned, he returns
to a traditional form of composition. The
surface is no longer completely covered by a
homogeneous web, but occupied instead
by a great dark fault amidst a clear mass
evoking an "interior" space that tends to
bury the image. Within this we notice how a
tear in a layer of white has a tendency to
cover the black, but also how a black mass
dispels the white or else pushes it into the
void it has created. A latent anguish is
perceived in this picture, executed at a time
of personal crisis for the painter. From then
on, his pictorial production would be
gradually reduced until the moment of his
death in 1956, never to attain the quality
characterising previous periods.

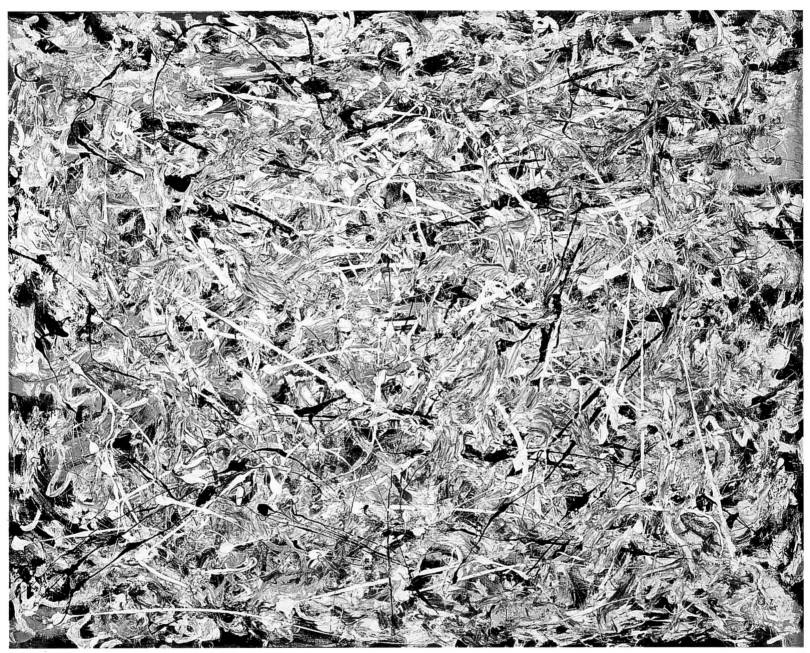

45 White Light, *1954.*
Oil, enamel and aluminium paint on canvas,
122.4 × 96.9 cm.
The Museum of Modern Art, New York.
The Sidney and Harriet Janis Collection.

List of Plates

1 Untitled (Self-Portrait), *1931–1935. Oil on gesso on canvas, mounted on fibreboard, 184 × 13.3 cm. L. S. Pollock Collection, New York.*

2 Untitled (Woman), *1935–1938. Oil on fibreboard, 35.8 × 26.6 cm. L. S. Pollock Collection, New York.*

3 Bird, *1938–1941. Oil and sand on canvas, 70.5 × 61.6 cm. The Museum of Modern Art, New York. Gift of Lee Krasner in memory of Jackson Pollock.*

4 Untitled (Circle), *1938–1941. Oil on gesso on fibreboard, 32.2 × 30.5 cm. The Museum of Modern Art, New York. Gift of Lee Krasner in memory of Jackson Pollock.*

5 Going West, *1934–1938. Oil on gesso on fibreboard, 38.3 × 52.7 cm. National Museum of American Art, Smithsonian Institution, Washington, D.C.*

6 The Flame, *1937. Oil on canvas, mounted on fibreboard, 51.1 × 76.2 cm. The Museum of Modern Art, New York. Enid A. Haupt Fund.*

7 Birth, *1938–1941. Oil on canvas, 116.4 × 55.1 cm. Tate Gallery, London.*

8 Untitled (Naked Man), *1938–1941. Oil on plywood, 127 × 60.9 cm. Private collection. Courtesy Robert Miller Gallery.*

9 Man, Bull, Bird, *1938–1941. Oil on canvas, 60.9 × 91.4 cm. The Anschutz Collection, Denver, Colorado.*

10 Stenographic Figure, *ca. 1942. Oil on linen, 101.6 × 142.2 cm. The Museum of Modern Art, New York. Mr. and Mrs. Walter Bareiss Fund.*

11 Male and Female, *ca. 1942. Oil on canvas, 184.4 × 124.5 cm. Philadelphia Museum of Art, Philadelphia. Gift of Mr. and Mrs. H. Gates Lloyd.*

12 The She-Wolf, *1943. Oil, gouache and plaster on canvas, 106.4 × 170.2 cm. The Museum of Modern Art, New York.*

13 The Moon-Woman Cuts the Circle, *ca. 1943. Oil on canvas, 109.5 × 104 cm. Musée national d'art moderne, Centre de Création Industrielle, Centre Georges Pompidou, Paris. Donated by Frank K. Lloyd, Paris, 1979.*

14 Guardians of the Secret, *1943. Oil on canvas, 122.9 × 191.5 cm. San Francisco Museum of Modern Art, San Francisco. Albert M. Bender Collection, Albert M. Bender Bequest Fund Purchase.*

15 The Water Bull (Accabonac Creek Series), *ca. 1946. Oil on canvas, 76.5 × 213 cm. Stedelijk Museum, Amsterdam.*

16 Alchemy, *1947. Oil, enamel, aluminium paint and string on canvas, 114.6 × 221.3 cm. Peggy Guggenheim Collection, Venice. The Solomon R. Guggenheim Foundation, New York.*

17 Eyes in the Heat (Sounds in the Grass Series), *1946. Oil on canvas, 137.2 × 109.2 cm. Peggy Guggenheim Collection, Venice. The Solomon R. Guggenheim Foundation, New York.*

18 Enchanted Forest, *1947. Oil on canvas, 221.3 × 114.6 cm. Peggy Guggenheim Foundation, Venice.*

19 Cathedral, *1947. Enamel and aluminium paint on canvas, 181.6 × 89 cm. Dallas Museum of Art, Dallas. Gift of Mr. and Mrs. Bernard J. Reiss.*

20 Full Fathom Five, *1947. Oil on canvas with nails, tacks, buttons, key, coins, cigarettes, matches, etc., 129.2 × 76.5 cm. The Museum of Modern Art, New York. Gift of Miss Peggy Guggenheim.*

21 Summertime, Number 9 A, 1948, *1948. Oil and enamel on canvas, 84.5 × 549.5 cm. Tate Gallery, London.*

22 Number 13 A, 1948: Arabesque, *1948. Oil and enamel on canvas, 94.6 × 295. 9 cm. Yale University Art Gallery, New Haven, Connecticut. Gift of Richard Brown Baker, B.A., 1935.*

23 The Wooden Horse: Number 10 A, 1948, *1948. Oil, enamel and wood hobbyhorse on brown cotton canvas, mounted on fibreboard, 90.1 × 190.5 cm. Moderna Museet, Stockholm.*

24 Number 26 A, 1948: Black and White, *1948. Enamel on canvas, 208 × 121.7 cm. Musée national d'art moderne, Centre de Création Industrielle, Centre Georges Pompidou, Paris.*

25 Silver over Black, Yellow and Red, *1948. Enamel on paper, pasted on canvas, 61 × 80 cm. Musée national d'art moderne, Centre de Création Industrielle, Centre Georges Pompidou, Paris.*

26 Number 13, 1949, *1949. Oil, enamel and aluminium paint on gesso on paper, mounted on fibreboard, 57.7 × 78.4 cm. Private collection.*

27 Number 10, 1949, *1949. Enamel and aluminium paint on canvas, mounted on wood, 45.7 × 272.4 cm. Museum of Fine Arts, Boston.*

28 Number 8, 1949, *1949. Oil, enamel and aluminium paint on canvas, 86.6 × 180.9 cm. Neuberger Museum of Art, Purchase College, State University of New York. Gift of Roy R. Neuberger.*

29 Number 3, 1949: Tiger, *1949. Oil, enamel, aluminium paint, string and cigarette fragment on canvas, mounted on fibreboard, 157.5 × 94.6 cm. Hirshhorn Museum and Sculpture Garden, Smithsonian Institution, Washington, D.C. Gift of the Joseph H. Hirshhorn Foundation, 1972.*

30 Number 4, 1949, *1949. Oil, enamel, aluminium paint and gravel on canvas, mounted on fibreboard, 90.5 × 87.3 cm. Yale University Art Gallery, New Haven.*

31 Number 32, 1950, *1950. Enamel on canvas, 269 × 457.5 cm. Kunstsammlung Nordthein Westfalen, Düsseldorf.*

32 Autumn Rhythm: Number 30, 1950, *1950. Oil on canvas, 267.7 × 525.8 cm. The Metropolitan Museum of Art, New York. George A. Hearn Fund, 1957.*

33 One: Number 31, 1950, *1950. Oil and enamel paint on canvas, 269.5 × 530.8 cm. The Metropolitan Museum of Art, New York.*

34 Lavender Mist: Number 1, 1950, *1950. Oil, enamel and aluminium paint on canvas, 221 × 299.7 cm. National Gallery of Art, Washington, D.C. Ailsa Mellon Bruce Fund.*

35 Black and White Polyptych, *1950. Oil on canvas, 60.9 × 203.2 cm. Mr. and Mrs. Arthur Rock.*

36 Number 11, 1951, *1951. Enamel on canvas, 146 × 352 cm. Daros Collection, Switzerland.*

37 Echo: Number 25, 1951, *1951. Enamel on canvas, 233.4 × 218.4 cm. The Museum of Modern Art, New York. Acquired through the Lillie P. Bliss Bequest and the Mr. and Mrs. David Rockefeller Fund.*

38 Brown and Silver II, *1951. Enamel and silver paint on unprimed canvas, 144.7 × 107.8 cm. Kunstmuseum Bern, Berne.*

39 Out of the Web, Number 7, *1949. Oil and enamel on fibreboard, 121.5 × 244 cm. Staatsgalerie Stuttgart, Stuttgart.*

40 Easter and the Totem, *1953. Oil on canvas, 208.6 × 147.2 cm. The Museum of Modern Art, New York. Gift of Lee Krasner in memory of Jackson Pollock.*

41 Blue Poles: Number II, 1952, *1952. Enamel and aluminium paint with glass on canvas, 210 × 486.8 cm. National Gallery of Australia, Canberra.*

42 Convergence: Number 10, 1952, *1952. Oil and enamel on canvas, 237.4 × 393.7 cm. Albright-Knox Art Gallery, Buffalo, New York. Gift of Seymour H. Knox, 1956.*

43 Portrait and a Dream, *1953. Oil on canvas, 148.6 × 342.2 cm. Dallas Museum of Art, Dallas. Gift of Mr. and Mrs. Algur H. Meadows and the Meadows Foundation, Incorporated.*

44 The Deep, *1953. Oil and enamel on canvas, 220.4 × 150.2 cm. Musée national d'art moderne, Centre de Création Industrielle, Centre Georges Pompidou, Paris. Donated by The Menil Foundation, Houston, 1975.*

45 White Light, *1954. Oil, enamel and aluminium paint on canvas, 122.4 × 96.9 cm. The Museum of Modern Art, New York. The Sidney and Harriet Janis Collection.*

Selected Bibliography

BERNARD HARPER FRIEDMAN, *Jackson Pollock: Energy Made Visible*, McGraw-Hill, New York, 1972.

HANS NAMUTH, *L'Atelier de Jackson Pollock*, Macula/Pierre Brochet, Paris, 1978. Essays by Rosalind Krauss and Francis V. O'Connor, and writings by Jackson Pollock.

FRANCIS VALENTINE O'CONNOR and EUGENE VICTOR THAW (eds.), *Jackson Pollock: A Catalogue Raisonnée of Paintings, Drawings, and Other Works*, Yale University Press, New Haven, 1978.

DENISE RIOUT et alt., *L'art des États-Unis*, Citadelles et Mazenod, Paris, 1992.

BARBARA ROSE, *Krasner/Pollock: A Working Relationship*, Guild Hall Museum, East Hampton, New York, 1981.

BERNICE ROSE, *Jackson Pollock: Drawing into Painting*, Musée d'Art Moderne de la Ville de Paris, Paris, 1979.

WILLIAM RUBIN, "Jackson Pollock illustrateur jungien: les limites de la critique psychologique", in *Jackson Pollock*, Centre Pompidou/MNAM, Paris, 1979.

IRVING SANDLER, *The Triumph of American Painting. A History of Abstract Expressionism*, Icon Edition, Harper & Row Publishers, New York, 1971.

DEBORAH SOLOMON, *Jackson Pollock: A Biography*, Simon & Schuster, New York, 1987.